Did You See That?

QUIPS, QUOTES AND ONE-LINERS

DERRIC JOHNSON

THOMAS NELSON PUBLISHERS
Nasvhille

Library of Congress Cataloging-in-Publication Data

Did you see that? / [compiled by] Derric Johnson.
    p. cm.
  ISBN 0-7852-4480-8
  1. Aphorisms and apothegms. 2. Quotations, English. I. Johnson, Derric, 1932–
II. Title.
PN6271.D53   2000
082—dc21   99–056225
                                                                   CIP

Printed in the United States of America
1 2 3 4 5 6 7 — 04 03 02 01 00

FIRST YOU HAVE TO GET THEIR ATTENTION

Have you ever seen a sign as you were driving down the road that made you laugh? Or one that made you think? Or one that made you look twice to be sure what it said?

This book contains thought-provoking sayings suitable for church signs, bulletins, sermons, newsletters, and more. The clever quips, quotes, and one-liners are a quick way to attract attention while leaving a lasting impression.

ATTITUDE

Winning is an inside job.

Those who complain about the way
the ball bounces . . . are usually
the ones who dropped it.

Let us live!
Let us love!
Let us share the
deepest secrets
of our souls!
You first.

Stress is what happens when your head says, "No" . . . But your mouth says, "Of course, I'd be glad to."

Those who make the worst use of their time . . . are the first to complain of its shortness.

There is a difference between perseverance and obstinacy . . . One is a strong will and the other is a strong won't.

Some men dream of worthy accomplishments . . . Others stay awake and make them happen.

We do not see things as they are . . . we see things as we are.

Sometimes it's hard to tell if you're carving yourself a niche . . . or digging yourself a hole.

The world is not interested in the storms you encountered . . . just if you brought in the ship.

Success comes before work only in the dictionary.

The biggest problem with being average is . . . you're as close to the bottom as you are to the top.

Life is a grindstone . . . whether it grinds you down or polishes you up depends on what you're made of.

If you think you can . . .
or think you can't . . .
you're probably right.

Too many people mistake their imagination for their memory.

If you need an expensive car or fancy clothes to make a statement about yourself . . . you don't have much to say.

Don't judge those who try and fail . . .
judge only those who fail to try.

No one grows old by living . . . only by losing interest in living.

Imagination was given to man to compensate him for what he is not . . . a sense of humor to console him for what he is.

When there's a piano to be moved . . . too many people are willing to carry the stool.

You can never be sure the stars are out of reach . . . unless you reach for them.

Even if you've been fishing for three hours and haven't gotten anything but a sunburn . . . you're still better off than the worm.

Even babies like to grab for things just beyond their reach.

Courage is often just ignorance of the facts.

Be thankful if you have a challenge a little harder than you like . . . a razor cannot be sharpened on a piece of velvet.

If you don't have time to do it right . . .
when will you have time to
do it over?

I always meant to become a procrastinator.

A conclusion is simply the place . . . where you got tired of thinking.

The one who says it cannot be done . . . should never interrupt the one who is doing it.

He who makes a mistake and fails to correct it . . . makes another.

Everybody is somebody else's weirdo.

CHANGE

Make change a choice.

What a frustrating day! I put five dollars in the change machine this morning . . . and I'm still me.

Everyone thinks of changing the world, but no one thinks of changing himself.

Don't ever pull a fence
down . . . until you know
the reason why it
was put up.

CHARACTER

Character consists of what you do on the third and fourth tries.

It may be that your sole purpose in life
is to serve as a warning to others.

If I take care of my character . . . my reputation will take care of itself.

Character is what God and the angels know of us . . . reputation is what men and women think of us.

Conscience is the inner voice that tells you . . . the IRS might audit your return.

There is no pillow as soft as a clear conscience.

EXCELLENCE

Excellence is never an accident.

If you want to have your dreams come true . . . you have to start by waking up.

There is no greater reason for excellence than ministry.

Improvement begins with "I."

The reason so many good ideas
die . . . is that they can't stand
solitary confinement.

To see things in a seed . . . that is vision.

EXPERIENCE

Experience is the name everyone gives to his mistakes.

A proverb is a short sentence based on long experience.

We learn from experience. Parents never wake up their second baby . . . just to see him smile.

Experience is the wisdom to recognize a mistake . . . when you make it again.

Learn from the mistakes of others . . . you don't have time to make them all yourself.

Smart people speak from experience . . . smarter people, from experience, do not speak.

FAITH

Faith makes things possible . . . not easier.

Of course we don't expect everyone to come to our church . . . Just you!

Hope sees the invisible . . . feels the intangible . . . and achieves the impossible.

Justice is getting what you deserve.
Mercy is not getting what
you deserve.
Grace is getting what you don't
deserve.

A church may be just what's
needed . . . when a "faith lift"
is required.

God loves you . . .
and I'm trying.

Too many people who only go to church occasionally expect a million-dollar answer . . . for a one-dollar contribution.

I never cease to be amazed at the strength of my weaknesses.

Jesus is coming . . .
Look busy!

Never fear shadows . . . they simply mean there's a light shining nearby.

God puts us in the dark . . . so we can see that he is the light.

What the caterpillar calls "the end" . . .
the butterfly calls "the beginning."

Patience is the ability to let your light shine after your fuse is blown.

FRIENDSHIP

A friend is someone who asks how you
are . . . and waits for the answer.

Be kind to your friends. If it weren't for them . . . you'd be a total stranger.

Only a friend can sympathize with your success.

Friends do good to and for each other . . . and never keep score.

It is never too soon to do a
kindness . . . because we
never know how soon
it will be too late.

Grudges are like live hand grenades . . . it's wise to release them before they destroy you.

To forgive calls upon our love. To forget calls upon our strength.

There are three things that grow more
precious with age . . .
old wood to burn, old books to
read, and old friends to enjoy.

True friendship prefers sincerity over praise . . . and loyalty over smiles.

True friendship is being more interested in listening to others . . . than in getting them to listen to you.

A true friend is someone who, when you've made a fool of yourself, doesn't think you've done a permanent job.

A friend not in need,
is a friend indeed.

If you lend a friend five dollars and never see him again . . . it was worth it.

He is a good friend . . . he speaks well of me behind my back.

Friends are the family . . . we choose for ourselves.

Greater love has no man than this, that he lay down his life for his friends.

—*Jesus Christ*

HOME & FAMILY

A home is four walls held together by love.

A happy home is where . . .
both mates think they
got better than
they deserve.

Marriage should be a duet . . . when one sings, the other claps.

Always remember that in the word "wedding" . . . "we" comes before "I."

Parental wisdom is bringing up your children . . . so that someone else will like them besides you.

Children are natural mimics. They act like their parents.

When we worry about what a child will be tomorrow . . . we sometimes forget that he is someone today.

People who wonder where the younger generation is headed . . . would do well to remember where it came from.

There's nothing thirstier than a child . . . who has just gone to bed.

The unbreakable toy is useful for breaking other toys.

Advice to teenagers: Leave home now . . . while you still know everything.

No matter how old a mother is . . .
she always watches her children for
signs of improvement.

HUMOR

He who laughs last . . . thinks slowest.

There are two ways to start a day . . . "Good morning, Lord." Or "Good Lord, it's morning."

Whether laughter is healthful or not . . . depends on the size of the person you're laughing at.

If you look like the photo on your drivers license . . . you aren't well enough to drive.

A reckless driver is a person who passes you on the highway . . . in spite of all you can do.

INSPIRATION

Always remember you are unique . . . just like everybody else.

A little experience can help a person overcome quite a bit of education.

Don't make the mistake of letting yesterday take up too much of today.

Eat one live frog the first thing in the morning . . . and nothing worse will happen to you for the rest of the day.

A closed mouth gathers no foot.

Nobody says "It's only a game" . . .
when his team is winning.

It's amazing to see how many people take ego trips . . . with so little luggage.

It's what you learn after you know it all that counts.

An optimist believes we live in the best of all possible worlds. The pessimist fears this is true.

Never forget to turn off the sound . . .
when your mind goes blank.

Some people are just like concrete . . .
thoroughly mixed up and
permanently set.

If it's true you are what you eat . . . order something rich.

When looking for a reason as to why things go wrong . . . never rule out sheer stupidity.

It requires wisdom to understand wisdom . . . music is nothing if the audience is deaf.

LIFE'S LESSONS

Never think you know it all.

Gossip travels with the speed of delight.

Silence can be an answer.

Tact is getting your point across
without sticking someone with it.

You're growing old gracefully when the number of things you can no longer do . . . is roughly equal to the number of things you no longer want to do.

It isn't necessary for a man to have his face lifted. If he's patient enough, it will grow up through his hair.

The secret is to become wise before you get old.

It seems as folks grow older . . . they often grow quieter. Maybe it's because they know much more to be quiet about.

It's nice to grow old . . . if you can stay young while you're doing it.

The toughest part of dieting isn't watching what you eat . . . it's watching what your friends eat.

LEADERSHIP

Knowledge cannot make us leaders . . .
but it can help us decide which leader to follow.

Some folks never seem to hear what
you say . . . unless you're saying
it to someone else.

Rain won't do any good unless the sun comes out . . . nor will criticism if there is no praise.

It's hard to know how far a branch will bend before it breaks.

Confidence is the feeling you have before you really understand the problem.

I used to be indecisive . . . but now I'm not so sure.

Authority can be assigned . . . but
respect must be earned.

If you can't be kind . . . at least have the decency to be vague.

If you try to improve another person by setting a good example . . . then you are really improving two people.

The right to be heard is constitutionally guaranteed. The right to be listened to must be earned.

LOVE

Age does not protect you from love . . . but love can protect you from age.

Love is a peculiar thing. In order to get it, you have to give it. And when you get it . . . you have to give it back to keep it.

As you look back upon your life, you will find that the moments when you have really lived . . . are the moments when you have done things in the spirit of love.

Enlightenment comes to the one who
changes from the love of power . . .
to the power of love.

MONEY

Money isn't everything. For instance . . . it isn't plentiful.

It used to be that a man who saved his money was a miser. Nowadays, he's a wonder.

If your outgo exceeds your income . . . your upkeep will become your downfall.

A fool and his money are
welcome everywhere.

A budget is a blueprint that shows you exactly which drain your money is going down.

It's hard to save money . . .
when your neighbors keep
buying things you
can't afford.

If you want to feel rich . . .
just count all of the
things you have . . . that
money can't buy.

Always remember . . . that the best
things in life aren't things.

SUCCESS

If at first you don't succeed . . . skydiving is not for you.

The great dividing line between success and failure can be expressed in five words . . . I DID NOT HAVE TIME!

Failures can be divided into two classes . . . those who thought and never did, and those who did and never thought.

Test pilots have a litmus test for evaluating problems. When something goes wrong, they ask, "Is this thing still flying?" If the answer is yes . . . then there's no immediate danger. There's no need to overreact.

We find comfort among those who agree with us . . . and growth among those who don't.

The highest reward for a man's toil is not what he gets for it . . . but what he becomes by it.

The real problem with your leisure time . . . is how to keep other people from using it.

Success seems to be largely a matter of hanging on . . . after others have let go.

Those who try to do something and fail . . . are infinitely better than those who try to do nothing . . . and succeed.

Losing options is one of life's greatest stresses.

When you don't know what
to do . . . walk fast and
look worried.

DID YOU SEE THAT?

Submit your favorite saying and win a book or CD-ROM.

Send us your church sign saying for our next book. If your entry is chosen, we will list your name and your saying and send you a copy of our next *Did You See That?* book.

All entries will have the opportunity to win a free *"Nelson Electronic Bible Reference Library,"* featuring the best of biblical reference materials on the market.

Please send your entries to:

Thomas Nelson, Inc.
Nelson Reference and Electronic
P.O. Box 141000
Nashville, TN 37214

ATTN: 2216